WNBA Hot Ticket

CHICAGO SKY

JOSH ANDERSON

Lerner Publications ◆ Minneapolis

To Leo and Dane, the biggest superstars I've ever met.

The stats and information in this book are accurate through the 2024 WNBA season.

Copyright © 2026 by Lerner Publishing Group, Inc.

All rights reserved. International copyright secured. No part of this book may be reproduced, stored in a retrieval system, or transmitted in any form or by any means—electronic, mechanical, photocopying, recording, or otherwise—without the prior written permission of Lerner Publishing Group, Inc., except for the inclusion of brief quotations in an acknowledged review.

Lerner Publications Company
An imprint of Lerner Publishing Group, Inc.
241 First Avenue North
Minneapolis, MN 55401 USA

For reading levels and more information, look up this title at www.lernerbooks.com.

Main body text set in Aptifer Slab LT Pro / Typeface provided by Linotype AG

Library of Congress Cataloging-in-Publication Data

Names: Anderson, Josh, author.
Title: Chicago Sky / Josh Anderson.
Description: Minneapolis, MN : Lerner Publications, 2025. | Series: WNBA hot ticket (Lerner sports) | Includes bibliographical references and index. | Audience: Ages 7–11 | Audience: Grades 2–3 | Summary: "With young superstars such as Angel Reese and Kamilla Cardoso, the Chicago Sky are one of the WNBA's most exciting teams. Explore the team's history and greatest moments"—Provided by publisher.
Identifiers: LCCN 2024046196 (print) | LCCN 2024046197 (ebook) | ISBN 9798765670118 (library binding) | ISBN 9798765683538 (paperback) | ISBN 9798765682173 (epub)
Subjects: LCSH: Chicago Sky (Basketball team)—History—Juvenile literature. | Women's National Basketball Association—Juvenile literature. | Women basketball players—United States—Juvenile literature.
Classification: LCC GV885.52.C47 .A534 2025 (print) | LCC GV885.52.C47 (ebook) | DDC 796.323/640977311—dc23/eng/20241224

LC record available at https://lccn.loc.gov/2024046196
LC ebook record available at https://lccn.loc.gov/2024046197

TABLE OF CONTENTS

INCREDIBLE COMEBACK. **4**

FACTS AT A GLANCE **5**

CHAPTER 1
CHICAGO'S TEAM **9**

CHAPTER 2
AMAZING STARS **15**

CHAPTER 3
BATTLE OF THE ROOKIES **21**

CHAPTER 4
A BRIGHT FUTURE. **27**

Glossary. 30
Learn More 31
Index 32

Chicago Sky player Candace Parker (*right*) looks for a way around the Phoenix Mercury's Brianna Turner (*left*) during the 2021 Finals.

INCREDIBLE COMEBACK

FACTS AT A GLANCE

- The Sky began play as an **EXPANSION TEAM** in 2006.
- The team won its first **WOMEN'S NATIONAL BASKETBALL ASSOCIATION (WNBA)** title in 2021.
- In 2024, rookie **ANGEL REESE** set the league record for most rebounds per game in a season with 13.1.
- Center **SYLVIA FOWLES** ranks second all-time in the WNBA for career rebounds.

Phoenix Mercury fans expected their team to win the 2021 WNBA Finals. But the Chicago Sky had taken a 2–1 lead in the series. They needed only one more victory to become champions for the first time.

Candace Parker had joined the Sky before the season. She wanted to bring a title to her hometown of Chicago, Illinois. The former WNBA Most Valuable Player (MVP) was nearing the end of her career. But she could still have a big impact on a game. With the Sky down 72–65 and just under five minutes left in the game, Parker stood near the three-point line with the ball.

Parker spotted Allie Quigley near the free-throw line. Quigley was the Sky's leading scorer in the series. Parker passed the ball to Quigley, who turned and shot. The ball went through the hoop to cut the Mercury's lead to five points.

Two minutes later, Parker dribbled fast up the court. Spotting two defenders charging toward her, Parker looked for an open teammate. As she reached the three-point line, she saw Kahleah Copper running toward the hoop. Parker threw a perfect bounce pass to Copper. Copper made the open layup. The play brought the Sky to within three points with less than three minutes remaining in the game.

Moments later, Parker received a pass from Sky point guard Courtney Vandersloot. Standing behind the three-point line, Parker shot the ball. The Chicago crowd went wild as the ball dropped through the hoop to tie the game 72–72.

After tying the game, the Sky kept scoring. They won the game 80–74. Although Parker had won a WNBA title earlier in her career, winning in her hometown was special. She was thrilled to help the Sky win Chicago's first WNBA title.

Allie Quigley made all 25 of her attempted free throws during the 2021 playoffs.

Candace Parker points up as she celebrates the Sky's first WNBA title in 2021.

The Chicago Sky's name honors the blue sky and bright sun of Chicago, located on the banks of Lake Michigan in Illinois.

CHAPTER 1
CHICAGO'S TEAM

The Chicago Sky began play as a WNBA expansion team during the 2006 season. The team's name and blue-and-yellow colors represent a beautiful Chicago day with a bright blue sky and yellow sunlight. Fans were excited to have a WNBA team in the city. But the Sky's first year was challenging on the court. The team won only five games in 2006.

Candace Parker signs a basketball for a fan after a 2022 home win at Wintrust Arena. The Sky have played home games there since 2018.

The Sky did not have a winning record in any of its first seven seasons. Although the team lost more than they won, they drafted two of their greatest players in team history during this period. In 2008, the Sky chose center Sylvia Fowles. Fowles played seven seasons in Chicago and was one of the game's top rebounders.

In 2011, Chicago drafted Courtney Vandersloot. Vandersloot played 12 seasons for the Sky. She became one of the best point guards in the history of women's basketball.

After making the playoffs for the first time in 2013, Vandersloot, Fowles, and young star Elena Delle Donne surprised many fans. Even though the Sky had a losing record during the 2014 season, they managed to reach the playoffs and went all the way to the WNBA Finals. They lost the Finals to the Phoenix Mercury. But the Sky's 2014 season was one of the most exciting in the team's history.

After 12 years in Chicago, Courtney Vandersloot (*center*) went on to win her second WNBA title with the New York Liberty.

Sylvia Fowles shoots over a Phoenix Mercury defender during the 2014 WNBA Finals.

The next time the Sky made the WNBA Finals was also unexpected. The Sky finished the 2021 season with a 16–16 record. This made Chicago one of the lowest-ranked teams to reach the playoffs that season. The Connecticut Sun had the league's best record with 26 wins. But the Sky defeated the Sun on their way to the Finals.

HOOPS SCOOP

In 2022, four Sky players were WNBA All-Stars. They were Kahleah Copper, Emma Meesseman, Candace Parker, and Courtney Vandersloot.

Angel Reese (*left*) accepts her Chicago Sky jersey from WNBA commissioner Cathy Engelbert (*right*) during the 2024 WNBA Draft.

The Sky's unlikely victory over the Phoenix Mercury in the Finals brought a title to Chicago for the first time. In 2024, the team picked power forward Angel Reese with the seventh overall pick in the WNBA draft. Reese's strong rookie season has given fans hope that another run to the Finals could be right around the corner.

SKY TAKES ACTION

Chicago Sky players dedicated the 2020 season to fighting for social justice and racial equality. They worked with local and national leaders to raise money for groups in Chicago such as the Movement for Black Lives and a local arts center. The team donated $10 for every point they scored, $100 for every win, and $50 for every loss to groups they felt helped the community the most. Players also auctioned game-worn items such as jerseys to raise more money that season.

Bringing their fans' attention to groups such as Black Lives Matter allows the Sky to make a difference in the Chicago area.

HOOPS SCOOP

Candice Dupree was the first member of the Sky to be chosen as an All-Star.

Candice Dupree dribbles past a Sacramento Monarchs defender during a 2008 game.

CHAPTER 2
AMAZING STARS

The Sky's top player during their early years was Candice Dupree. Dupree played four seasons in Chicago from 2006 to 2009. In three of those seasons, the WNBA chose Dupree as an All-Star. Dupree led the Sky in scoring during three of her four seasons with the team.

In 2008, the Sky picked center Sylvia Fowles second overall in the WNBA Draft. Fowles became one of the best defenders and rebounders in league history. She played seven seasons in Chicago.

Fowles won the WNBA's Defensive Player of the Year award four times. The league chose Fowles as an All-Star eight times. Her 4,006 rebounds are the second-most in WNBA history.

Sylvia Fowles (*right*) blocks a shot from the Phoenix Mercury's Penny Taylor (*center*) during the 2014 WNBA Finals.

Courtney Vandersloot joined the Sky in 2011. She played 12 seasons in Chicago. During that time, the WNBA picked her as an All-Star four times. A slick passer, Vandersloot has led the league in assists five times in her career. Her 2,849 assists rank second all-time.

Allie Quigley signed with the Sky in 2013 and played 10 seasons in Chicago. During that time, Quigley won the Sixth Player of the Year award twice. She was the best player in the league who started most games on the bench. Quigley's 3,723 points for the Sky are the most in team history.

Courtney Vandersloot (*left*) and Allie Quigley (*right*) combined for 6,873 points during the 10 seasons they played together for the Sky.

While Elena Delle Donne only played four seasons in Chicago, they were great seasons. The forward won the league's Rookie of the Year award in 2013. Two seasons later, she averaged 23.4 points per game and was named the league's MVP. Delle Donne helped the Sky to their first WNBA Finals in 2014.

Elena Delle Donne dribbles around DeWanna Bonner of the Phoenix Mercury during the 2014 WNBA Finals.

Kahleah Copper played seven seasons for the Sky from 2017 to 2023. The WNBA chose Copper as an All-Star three times during this period. She averaged 17 points per game in the 2021 Finals and was named Finals MVP.

The Sky picked Angel Reese seventh overall in the 2024 WNBA Draft. Reese quickly became the team's best player and the WNBA's top rebounder. As a rookie, she broke the league record for most double-doubles in a row.

Kahleah Copper scored 2,677 points and grabbed 799 rebounds during her seven seasons with the Sky.

Angel Reese finished the 2024 season with 462 points and 63 assists for the Sky.

Reese had a double-double when she scored 10 or more points and grabbed at least 10 rebounds in a game. She did this 15 times in a row. She also set a rookie record with 20 rebounds in three straight games.

Before a wrist injury ended her rookie season, Reese grabbed her 446th rebound. She broke the WNBA single-season record set by Sylvia Fowles in 2018 for most rebounds in a single season. A'ja Wilson of the Las Vegas Aces broke Reese's record a few weeks later. But Reese still leads the WNBA in most rebounds per game in a season with 13.1.

Angel Reese (*right*) and the Louisiana State University Tigers defeated Caitlin Clark (*left*) and the Iowa Hawkeyes in the 2023 college national championship.

CHAPTER 3
BATTLE OF THE ROOKIES

The 2024 WNBA Draft was packed with future superstars. After a record-breaking college career, Caitlin Clark was picked first overall by the Indiana Fever. Most fans expected Clark to be the league's top rookie. Largely because of Clark, there was more interest in the WNBA than ever before.

Clark and Angel Reese had been rivals in college, and their rivalry continued in the WNBA. While Clark had a great rookie season, Reese set records of her own in 2024. The first two matchups between the league's top rookies did not go well for Reese and the Sky. The teams first faced off in June 2024. Reese finished with eight points and 13 rebounds, but the Fever beat the Sky 71–70.

Angel Reese (*left*) and Caitlin Clark (*right*) show that even rivals can be friends at the 2024 WNBA Draft.

Later that month, the teams played again. Clark had one of her best games of the season. She finished with 23 points, eight rebounds, and nine assists. The Fever won again 91–83.

By the third matchup between the teams, Reese had begun to receive more attention from fans and media covering the league. But she still hadn't led the Sky to victory over Clark and the Fever. About halfway through the fourth quarter, the Fever held an 82–70 lead. It looked like the Sky would fall to the Fever again. But Reese was determined not to let another matchup with her rival slip away. She scored to cut the lead to 10.

Angle Reese (*left*) watches for a chance to steal the ball from Caitlin Clark (*right*) during a 2024 game.

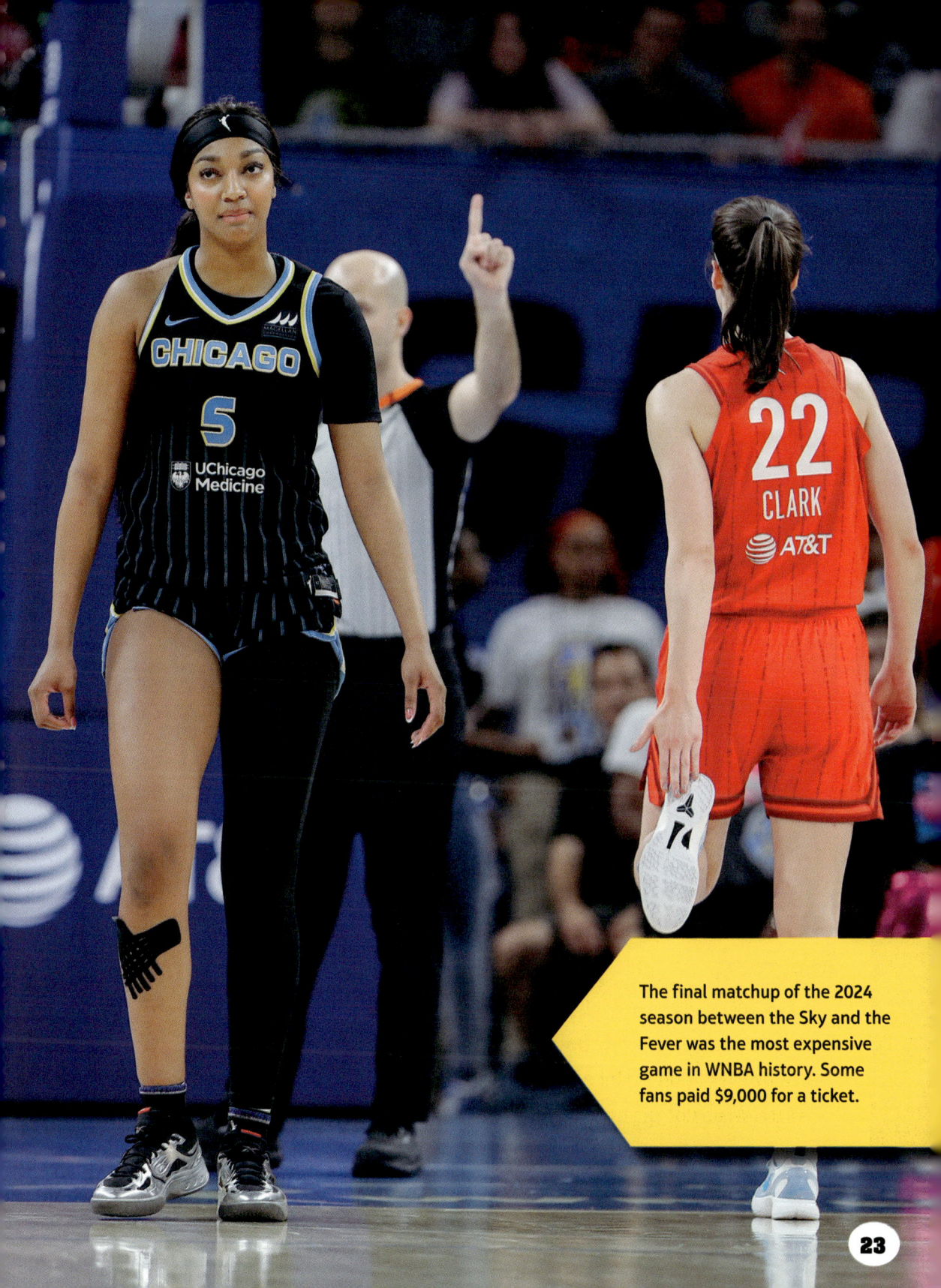

The final matchup of the 2024 season between the Sky and the Fever was the most expensive game in WNBA history. Some fans paid $9,000 for a ticket.

A minute later, Reese hit another basket that cut the lead to five. With a little more than three minutes left, Reese scored again and was fouled. Her free throw tied the game 82–82.

With under a minute left and the game tied 84–84, Reese drove toward the hoop for a left-handed basket to give the Sky an 86–84 lead. Reese finished the game with a career-best 25 points. She also grabbed 16 rebounds. For the first time that season, the Sky defeated the Fever 88–87.

Caitlin Clark (*right*) guards Angel Reese (*left*) during the first matchup of the season between the two teams.

HOOPS SCOOP

Courtney Vandersloot is the team's all-time steals leader with 457.

Angel Reese (*right*) grabbed 53 rebounds across four games against the Indiana Fever during the 2024 season.

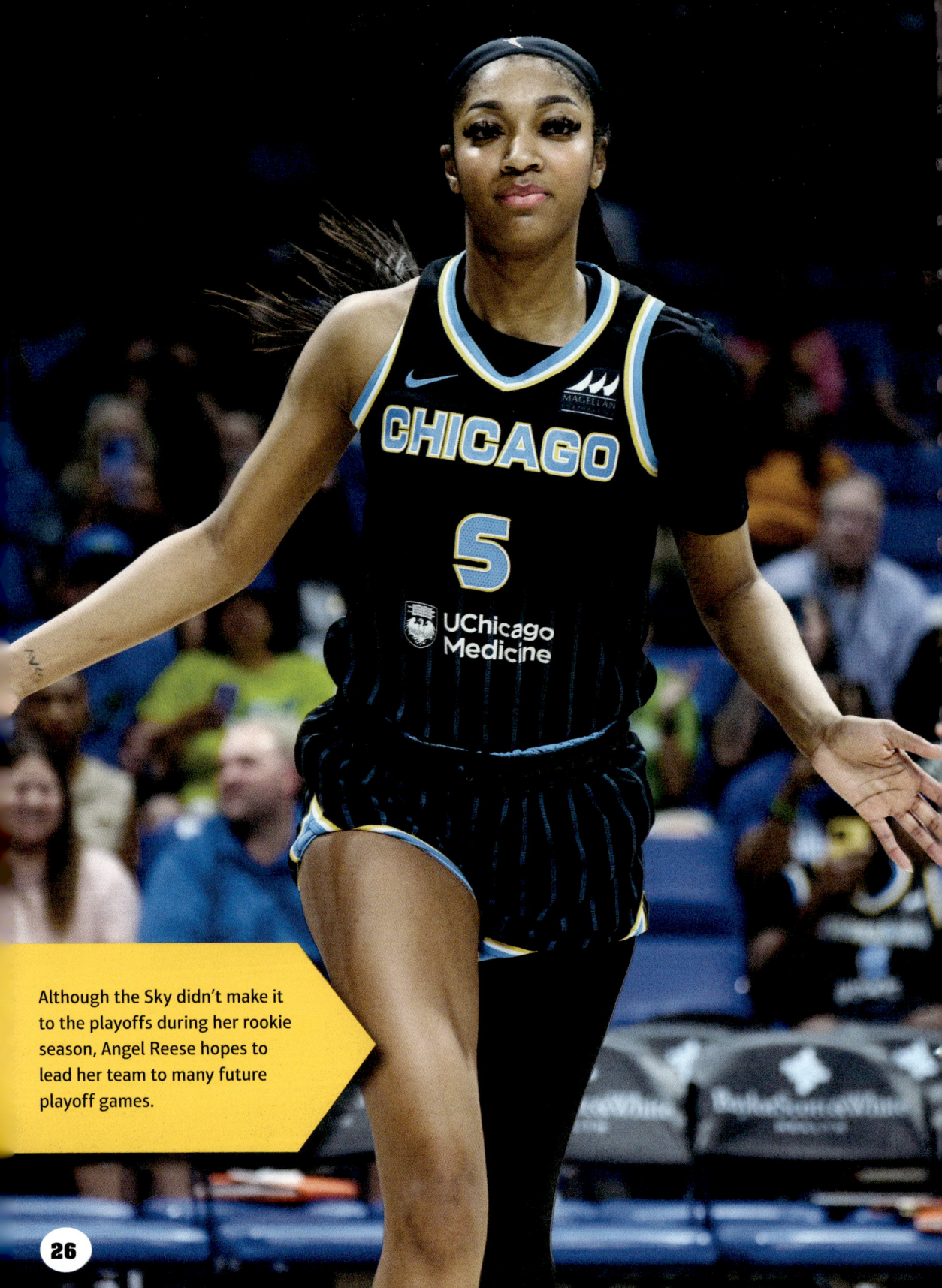

Although the Sky didn't make it to the playoffs during her rookie season, Angel Reese hopes to lead her team to many future playoff games.

CHAPTER 4
A BRIGHT FUTURE

The 2024 addition of superstar Angel Reese has added extra excitement to Sky basketball. But the team is still adjusting to the loss of several key players in recent years. All-time leading scorer Allie Quigley, All-Stars Courtney Vandersloot and Kahleah Copper, and future Hall of Famer Candace Parker all left the team between 2022 and 2024.

The departure of Kahleah Copper (*left*), Candace Parker (*center*), and Allie Quigley (*right*) left the Sky with a clean slate and a chance to rebuild the team with new talent.

In 2024, the Chicago Sky was a team with a lot of young talent. Although Reese got more headlines as a rookie, the Sky chose center Kamilla Cardoso four picks earlier than Reese in the 2024 WNBA Draft. Cardoso is one of the taller players in the league at 6-foot-7 (2 m) and made a big impact as a rookie. The team also added top scorer Chennedy Carter in 2024. She has averaged more than 14 points per game in her career.

Thanks to rookie sensations including Caitlin Clark and Angel Reese, fan interest in the WNBA is higher than ever. The Sky's challenge will be getting skilled young players to work together as a unit. If they can succeed, the Sky may soon find themselves making a deep playoff run once again—and Chicago fans will be watching.

Chennedy Carter (left) and Angel Reese (right) talk during a 2024 game.

Kamilla Cardoso finished the 2024 season with the second-most rebounds for the Sky with 254.

GLOSSARY

All-Star: a player chosen as one of the best in league to compete in a game against other top players

assist: a pass that leads directly to a basket

auction: to sell items to people who offer to pay the most money

Basketball Hall of Fame: a museum in Springfield, Massachusetts, that honors the best basketball players and coaches

double-double: when a player reaches at least 10 in two different stats in a game

expansion team: a team added to an existing sports league

free throw: an open shot taken from behind a set line after a foul by an opponent

rebound: when a player grabs and controls the ball after a missed shot

rival: a player or team that tries to defeat or be more successful than another

rookie: a first-year player

title: championship

WNBA Draft: when WNBA teams take turns choosing new players

LEARN MORE

Chicago Sky
https://sky.wnba.com/

Doeden, Matt. *G.O.A.T. Women's Basketball Teams*. Minneapolis: Lerner Publications, 2021.

Thompson, Kim. *Angel Reese*. Mankato, MN: Amicus Learning, 2025.

Whiting, Jim. *The Story of the Chicago Sky*. Mankato, MN: Creative Education and Creative Paperbacks, 2024.

WNBA
https://www.wnba.com/

Women's National Basketball Association Facts for Kids
https://kids.kiddle.co/Women%27s_National_Basketball_Association

INDEX

Cardoso, Kamilla, 28
Carter, Chennedy, 28
Clark, Caitlin, 21–22, 28
Copper, Kahleah, 6, 12, 18, 27

Delle Donne, Elena, 10, 17
Dupree, Candice, 14–15

Fowles, Sylvia, 5, 10, 15, 19

Meesseman, Emma, 12

Parker, Candace, 5–6, 12, 27

Quigley, Allie, 6, 16, 27

Reese, Angel, 5, 12, 18–19, 21–22, 24, 27–28

Vandersloot, Courtney, 6, 10, 12, 16, 25, 27

WNBA Draft, 12, 15, 18, 21, 28
WNBA Finals, 5, 10–11, 17

PHOTO ACKNOWLEDGMENTS

Image credits: Jonathan Daniel/Getty Images, p.4; M. Anthony Nesmith/Icon Sportswire/Getty Images, p.6; Stacy Revere/Getty Images, p.7; Raymond Boyd/Michael Ochs Archives/Getty Images, p.8; Michael Reaves/Getty Images, p. 9; Jennifer Stewart/Getty Images, p.10; Christian Petersen/Getty Images, p.11; Sarah Stier/Getty Images, p.12; Julio Aguilar/Getty Images, p.13; Greg Ashman/Cal Sport Media/Getty Images, p.14; Jennifer Stewart/Getty Images, p.15; Ethan Miller/Getty Images, p.16; Jonathan Daniel/Getty Images, p.17; Quinn Harris/Getty Images, p.18; Emilee Chinn/Getty Images, p.19; Andy Lyons/Getty Images, p.20; Cora Veltman/Sportico/Getty Images, p.21; Emilee Chinn/Getty Images, p.22; Melissa Tamez/Icon Sportswire/Getty Images, p.23; Brian Spurlock/Icon Sportswire/Getty Images, p.24; Andy Lyons/Getty Images, p.25; Cooper Neill/Getty Images, p.26; Scott Taetch/Getty Images, p.27; Melissa Tamez/Icon Sportswire/Getty Images, p.28; Geoff Stellfox/Getty Images, p. 29

Cover image: Sports Press Photo/Shaina Benhiyoun/SPP/Sipa USA/Newscom